Scattered Reflections

Beginnings and ends
Musings from the soul
Adrift in the wind

Lynn Long

ISBN: 978-93-6354-050-7

First Edition: 2024
Rs. 200/-

Cyberwit.net
HIG 45 Kaushambi Kunj, Kalindipuram
Allahabad - 211011 (U.P.) India
http://www.cyberwit.net
Tel: +(91) 9415091004
E-mail: info@cyberwit.net

Printed at Repro India Limited.

Dedication

To every soul

who hears the calling of

whispers

upon the wind

I dedicate these words to you

The Muse Within…

And to Tasha

Whose beautiful soul

touched my heart

with hers

Raising the bar high

Forever she inspires

Contents

All is Never Lost

Adrift in thoughts
Floating on air
All is never truly
lost
Just enfolded with
care

I loved you like Purple

Thoughts are random
Memories are true
And somewhere in between
There's always been you
For the moon needs
no muse
to shine bright
Only the promise of love
amid a lavender sky

And I loved you
like purple =ØœÜ
in twilight hues

If Only

I wanted to write you
a poem
Perhaps about the moon
lulling me to sleep
Or the stars in which
I dream…
Alas, the morning sun
took my words
His beauty
A silence
Only my soul heard
I would write you a poem
If only my words could
make their way home

The Crescent Moon

Nestled upon the
leaves of a sleeping tree
Is the crescent moon
Dreaming awake

The crescent moon
One with my heart
Rising too soon
A light in the dark

Dear Moon

Dear Moon
Your light inspires
Illuminating the night
Freeing my soul
Come shine upon me
In memories of old
Guide the path
Embraced at last

The Night

Nights are never lonely
beneath the shimmering moon
For there is where I lie awake
Lost ...in thoughts of you

Weary is the soul
Seeking the light
For the dreamer
Still dreams
In spite of the night

Yearnings from the Heart

Distant moon
Amid the ebony sky
In your love
I still fall
Night after night

In words unspoken
Wished upon the stars
The moon heard
Her yearnings from the
heart

A Star Waits for You

He is but a dream
He sleeps with the moon

From the moon he sees
She is starlight and summer blooms
All he ever needs

Can you love someone
And still wish upon the Moon
Knowing all the while
A Star waits for you

I See you in Dream

We've never met you and I
And I love you already
I've always loved you
I know this now
All the dreams
The love songs
The seeking
You've always been
How can it be
For we've never met
Yet, I see you in dream

Poetry Undone

Never will we know-
what may have been
For only remnants of
our words ...linger
Upon the wind
Caressing the soul softly
In a love song
Once written
Alas, unsung
Her heart still waits
Poetry undone

Awry

I should be kissing
Stars and dancing
with the **Moon**
Yet, once again
I find myself
Awry
In loving you

Hello

You feel like a stranger
Your words-
hollow and cold
Someone with whom
I've barely said ...hello
Surely, not the shining
star
I once knew
Illuminating
A crystalline sky
As you opened moon petals
In the coming sunrise

The Heart Still Beats Strong

I always knew the heart,
vast beyond measure
could love even whilst broken,
but this, this shattering of pieces
carried on the breeze
…is even more than I can believe
Yet, the heart still beats strong
A reminder to carry on-
and to never stop falling

I never knew
The depth in which
my heart grew
Until it stopped …loving you

Destined as Fate

Time keeps moving
Still we wait
In the shadows of memory
Destined as fate
Two stars on a journey
Falling from the sky
The promise of forever
A truth in the lie
For lost is the key
Unlocking the heart
Ever to meet
Always to part
Time keeps moving
Still we wait
In the shadows of memory
Destined as fate
A parallel universe
Written in the stars
Two souls on a journey
Lovers from afar
Our story un-ended
A fairytale bliss
Ever we meet
To part in a kiss

Falling in Love

(Acrostic Poem)
Falling into you
A sweet reverie
Lost in a truth
Landing on a breeze
Into you I escape
No longer afraid
Gravity beckons
Illuminated by your light
No longer my own
Lovers in flight
Oh bittersweet ache
Veering still I fall
Eternally in your wake

Illuminated Reverie

Will you catch me when I fall
Teetering the celestial abyss
Where starseeds fly
And lovers kiss…

A light in the shadows
A wish in the dark
Illuminated reverie
Musings from the heart

His Light

Night touches day
In need of his light
For his light a warmth
She's never known
Enraptured she finds
His world ...is home

For you who shines amidst sunbeams
Could you ever love me-
A dreamer beneath the
moon

My Muse

Words ebb and flow
With the tides I watch them go
From me to you and back again
You are my muse...
My sometimes friend
And when we speak
My heart awakes
A floods released
Words cascade
Into the river far below
Spilling forth, they free the soul
Alas, my words will have to keep
As silence takes me back to sleep
Adrift in dream I await
For my muse-
Ever late...

Who Will be Found

As I wander in dream
Searching for you
Often I'm lost
Between real and truth
For there lies the space
In which my heart
resides
A place of longing
deep inside
And I wonder …as I wander
Who will be found
The soul ever seeking-
or the heart ever bound

The Journey

Though we travel
the same road
Beneath the same
vast gray sky
Our journeys differ
...you and I
For my path follows
the reticent dance
of raindrops
And yours-
the thunderous
roar of a summer
storm

Asleep

I once was a butterfly
My wings the color of honey
I flew with the wind
My world vast
Endless in possibility
And I dreamed
Anew
Awakening with the dawn
Sleeping to the thunder
Alas, time, also endless
Changed my world within
And I didn't know
Couldn't know
I would transform- yet again
The metamorphosis ever painful
The journey brand new
I once was a butterfly
Asleep
In her cocoon

Breathe

There are days when
I feel so lost
I cannot find
my way
Trapped beneath a sea
of doubt
Anchored against the
waves
I scream and shout
No one hears
My deepest thoughts
My truest fears
And on those days
When I'm lost
at sea
I take a deep
breath
and remember me

Depths Unknown

Afloat beneath a cobalt sky
Where lavender hues
Kiss mountain highs
I sail to depths
unknown
Embracing new horizons
With the tides ebb and flow

Longing for a Summer Wind

Reflecting on what has
always been
What forever shall be
Languidly I linger
Longing for a summer wind
To whisk my spirit away
Upon its gentle breeze
As I share whispered
secrets amongst the clouds
and trees…
xxxxxxxxxxxxxxxxx
Jade petals
Iridescent on the vine
Stopping to smell the Jasmine
I lose to time

Floating on a Nebulous

Floating on a nebulous
Adrift in contemplation
Teetering at the precipice
I wander the constellations
Surfing celestial infinity
Riding on waves of euphoria
Swimming in sublimity
No longer lost in moria
For I'm chillin' with the hatter
Sippin' tea with honey
Where time never matters
Unless you ask the bunny

Flow

A river at heart
Ever-changing
Yet ... the same
Flowing to the sea

In times of uncertainty
In times of woe
Be as the river
And simply ...flow

Raindrops of moments

Caught up in reverie
Forgetting the mundane
Lavender evokes
Like a bubble of champagne
Wandering on pause
Days without end
Raindrops of moments
Cast to the wind

The Universe Within

The universe within empowers
my divine goddess
Freeing the soul
She enlightens
inner peace and strength
Her incandescent energy
intense with love
brings a freedom
beyond any I have ever known
And like the moon-
illuminating from afar
She is one with my heart

And the Moon has Wings

White hibiscus
Falling rain
Butterfly kisses
And the moon
has wings

Purple haze
Midnight blue
And she gazes upon
the world
Through eyes brand new

The Ibis fly
Amid starlit blooms
And she sits on a
mountain
Empowered in
truth

Summer

Finding ground in the sticky
heat of summer
I hear the thud, its sound familiar
As ripened mangoes in shades of gold
Fall one after another
Loosened from the aging
branches of a once youthful tree
And I think ... perhaps
They are free

Forgotten Truth

The flies still buzz
though nothing remains
Where the lizards lie
beneath the mango tree
And I'm not sure just
what it all means
This maddening bliss
torn apart at the seams
This reflection of woe
in letting go
Yet, isn't it happy
and a bit sad too
The realization-
we're all but a memory
Of a forgotten truth

Time Effervescent

Memories of childhood
For me, a blur…
A contortion of thoughts
Rooms larger in my child's mind
Filled with music and light
And shadows too.
Hidden in plain sight
Where a thinly disguised veil often hung…
Casually draped over the windows and
above the doors
A remnant of youth
I carry with me
Alas, all that is seen is never truly as it seems
And though the veil disguised remained
There awaited a magical place
Just beyond its reach
Lined with citrus and magnolia trees
Beckoning with the first rays of dawn
I can still remember sitting beneath those trees
The feelings of innocence shared
with friends and siblings- as we told stories
and took swigs from a soda bottle
Germs… never a forefront of thought in our minds
Dreaming of future worlds
Knowing we'd someday leave this one behind
And time… effervescent as bubbles
in Ginger Ale
Escaping without our consent

Watching the World Passing By

Dreaming of better days
Outside my windowsill
I watch the world pass by
Learning to embrace change
…still

Time ever keeping
Present entwines past
The fork in the road
All too clear
Yet I linger on the path
Watching the world passing by
Just within my grasp

And I am tired
Caught up in the throes
Lost in the why
Dreaming of better days
Outside my windowsill
And I don't think they're coming
Watching the world passing by
xxxxxxxxxxxxxxx
The present lost
is time missed
For the moment
ceases to exist

From Dawn to Twilight

Sometimes I wonder
If the girl of yesterday
Would understand
The woman of today

From dawn to twilight
A role I play
With the coming of night
I leave the day
For in the moon's soft glow
I awaken in dream
True to my soul
I'm all I believe

Soaring high
The dragon flies
Finding in hope
She can touch the sky

Fragments

Sunlight flickers
Yellow and gold
In the shadows
of memories
Her forgotten soul
Fragments
Adrift upon gossamer wings
She now dances with butterflies
On an Autumn breeze

Outside the Window

Honeysuckles red
Adorn leaves of green
Outside the window
Where often she dreams
No need for rainbows
Amid the sage and thyme
For hers is a world
Spoken in rhyme

The Wildflower

The Awakening of her soul
didn't happen in the resounding
of fireworks illuminating the ebony
sea-
Instead, it came in the watering of a wildflower
growing by the roadside
Wilting in the heat of a hot summer sun
Often overlooked by the many passersby
Told to let it be- for it will either flourish
or it will die…
But where they saw a weed,
she saw hope
and beauty
Alive
And so she watered the hope
growing by the roadside
Wilting in the heat of a hot summer sun
And she watched it flourish.
And she watched it bloom.
And its blossom became a tree
And the many passersby
Who only saw a weed
Marveled at the beauty
Alive
Where once overlooked
Left to flourish …or to die

Dreamscape

And the rain falls
softly
In a gentle caress of my soul
A beautiful reminder
of the love within
amid the feel of
raindrops
upon my skin
Its steady tempo
A constant
On this cloudy day
As I sip warm tea
Beneath a sky of gray
Thunder rumbles
A faraway tune
I hear the calling
And I fall too
Down the rabbit hole
Of forgotten reverie
Where fluorescent hues
In shades of green
Tint the landscape
Reminiscent in dream

For I've been here before
Have felt its familiar pang
Walked the many corridors
Only to turn back again
xxxxxxxxxxxxxxxxxxxxxxxxxx

I suppose I will always visit in dream

Alternate Dream

Sky aglow in wonder
Celestial infinity
Forever… a mere moment
Basking in fragility
Wandering, but not lost
Seeking, but still not found
Reaching for a distant star
Eternally bound
Luminous is the shining light
Not unlike my own
Gleaming in the distance
A place …called home
Wandering, but not lost
Seeking, but still not found
I ponder the alternate dream
Adrift amid its sound
The music a hushed lullaby
One with my heart
Entwining the soul-
to a timeless love…
Parallel worlds apart
Wandering, but not lost
Seeking, but still not found
Illuminating is the distant star
Eternally bound

Hear the Koto Sing

Caught up in the nine to five
Still seeking the sustainable dream
Entwining the two…
A spider's web of deceit
For time ever moving
A vortex in the abyss
of one's soul
Alas, mere perception
Pauses in the creative flow
Like a lasso to the moon
The kraken's tentacle pulls
Gravity beckons
And for just a moment
I've lost the muse
Yet, the artist within still resides
Dancing the wanton path
Waltzing high
In homage to reverie
A symphony at play
Time ever present
Hear the Koto sing
Hidden hues still sought
Amid the barren plains
Splashes of color
Upon a blank canvas
of dreams…

Reflections

Silver diamonds
Mere reflections upon
the window pane
Thunder resounds
Yet the world still sleeps
Raindrops fall from an ashen sky
And I want to be- as the silver diamonds
One with night
Illuminating the ebony sea
Luminescent ...and free

I am the Muse

Wildflowers
The setting sun
And a journey
of the heart
just begun

For I am the dreamer
The muse within
Writing on moon beams
My story begins

www.ingramcontent.com/pod-product-compliance
Ingram Content Group UK Ltd.
Pitfield, Milton Keynes, MK11 3LW, UK
UKHW041316190726
13845UKWH00025B/318

9 789363 540507